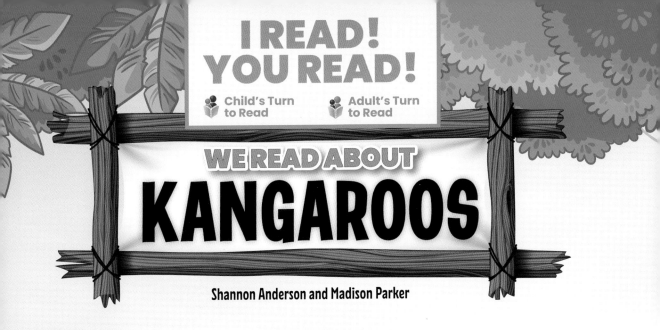

I READ! YOU READ!

Child's Turn to Read **Adult's Turn to Read**

WE READ ABOUT

KANGAROOS

Shannon Anderson and Madison Parker

Table of Contents

SEAHORSE PUBLISHING

Parent and Caregiver Guide

Reading aloud with your child has many benefits. It expands vocabulary, sparks discussion, and promotes an emotional bond. Research shows that children who have books read aloud to them have improved language skills, leading to greater school success.

I Read! You Read! books offer a fun and easy way to read with your child. Follow these guidelines.

Before Reading

- Look at the front and back covers. Discuss personal experiences that relate to the topic.
- Read the *Words to Know* at the back of the book. Talk about what the words mean.
- If the book will be challenging or unfamiliar to your child, read it aloud by yourself the first time. Then, invite your child to participate in a second reading.

During Reading

CHILD

Have your child read the words beside this symbol. This text has been carefully matched to the reading and grade levels shown on the cover.

ADULT

You read the words beside this symbol.

- Stop often to discuss what you are reading and to make sure your child understands.
- If your child struggles with decoding a word, help them sound it out. If it is still a challenge, say the word for your child and have them repeat it after you.
- To find the meaning of a word, look for clues in the surrounding words and pictures.

After Reading

- Praise your child's efforts. Notice how they have grown as a reader.
- Use the *Comprehension Questions* at the back of the book.
- Discuss what your child learned and what they liked or didn't like about the book.

Most importantly, let your child know that reading is fun and worthwhile. Keep reading together as your child's skills and confidence grow.

KANGAROOS

CHILD

A zoo is a fun place to see animals and learn about them.

One animal you may find in a zoo is a kangaroo.

ADULT

A zoo is a type of park where many kinds of animals live. Zoos help protect the animals inside them.

These large leapers are built to bounce.

They have big feet and strong back legs.

Long tails help them balance.

CHILD

Jumping is easy for kangaroos. Jumping helps kangaroos travel long distances without using too much energy.

ADULT

Kangaroo tails can grow to be four feet (one meter) long!

Kangaroos can jump fast and far.

They can leap the length of a school bus in one big hop!

CHILD

A school bus can be up to 40 feet (12 meters) long. The longest recorded animal jump was 43 feet (13 meters) by a red kangaroo.

ADULT

Kangaroos are **marsupials**.

They have pouches to help them carry and feed their babies.

Like all **marsupials**, kangaroos are mammals. Mammals are vertebrates, which means they have a backbone. They also have hair or fur and make milk for their babies.

Baby kangaroos are called **joeys**.

When joeys are born, they are only about one inch (three centimeters) long.

CHILD

The word **joey** may come from an ancient language spoken by Australian Aboriginal peoples. It means "little animal."

ADULT

If there is danger, a joey runs to get in its mom's pouch.

Newborn joeys climb into their mom's pouch.

They stay in the pouch to drink milk and grow for around nine months.

A joey does not leave its mom's pouch at all until it is four months old. Then, it comes out for short periods of time to practice walking and exploring.

Kangaroos are **herbivores**.

They eat grass, leaves, and flowers.

Herbivores eat only plants. They don't eat meat. Carnivores eat only meat. Omnivores eat both plants and meat.

Kangaroos live in groups called **mobs**.

CHILD

There are many different kinds of kangaroos.

Many kangaroo **mobs** have 50 or more animals.
Some types of kangaroos are eastern kangaroos,
western grey kangaroos, and red kangaroos.

ADULT

Some kangaroos live in trees.
Some live underground!

In the wild, kangaroos live for six to ten years.

They can live to be 20 years old in zoos.

CHILD

Kangaroos live longer in zoos because they are cared for and protected. Zookeepers make sure that kangaroos get the food they need to stay healthy.

ADULT

Most kangaroos live in **Australia**.

If you cannot go to Australia to see kangaroos, you can find them at the zoo!

Wild kangaroos live all over the continent of **Australia**. They like flat, open plains where they can find tasty grasses and shrubs to eat.

Words to Know

Australia (aw-STRAIL-yuh): one of Earth's continents; the continent that is south and east of Asia

herbivores (HUR-buh-vors): animals that eat only plants

joeys (JOH-eez): baby kangaroos

marsupials (mahr-SOO-pee-ulz): animals that carry their babies in pouches on their abdomens

mobs (mahbs): groups of kangaroos

Index

Comprehension Questions

1. What are baby kangaroos called?
    a. joeys   b. pouch pals   c. jumpers

2. What would kangaroos like to eat?
    a. wild dogs and foxes
    b. leaves and flowers
    c. lizards and snakes

3. A group of kangaroos is called a ___.
    a. flock   b. herd   c. mob

4. True or False: Kangaroos can jump the length of a school bus.

5. True or False: Kangaroos live all over the world.

Written by: Shannon Anderson and Madison Parker
Design by: Under the Oaks Media
Editor: Kim Thompson

Library of Congress PCN Data
We Read About Kangaroos / Shannon Anderson and Madison Parker
I Read! You Read!
ISBN 979-8-8873-5308-1 (hard cover)
ISBN 979-8-8873-5393-7 (paperback)
ISBN 979-8-8873-5478-1 (EPUB)
ISBN 979-8-8873-5563-4 (eBook)
Library of Congress Control Number: 2023930202

Printed in the United States of America.

Photographs/Shutterstock: Karen Brough: cover, p. 13; Alex Godoy
Photography: p. 3; Martin Pelanek: p. 5; Kevin Wells Photography:
p. 6-7; Adele Heidenreich: p. 8; Timothy Christianto: p. 11; Kjuurs:
p. 12; Benny Morty: p. 15; Katarina Christenson: p. 16; Simash
Photography: p. 17; Oleg Mayorov: p. 19; Pyty: p. 20 (map); Pawel
Papis: p. 20; Davesayit: p. 21

Seahorse Publishing Company

www.seahorsepub.com

Published in the United States
Seahorse Publishing
PO Box 771325
Coral Springs, FL 33077